the magic of Crystals

Front cover: *Clear quartz cluster (Arkansas, USA)*

Previous page: *Aqua aura (Arkansas, USA)*

Opposite page: *Clear quartz generators with clear quartz and hematite polished stones (Brazil)*

the magic of Crystals

Wendy Jones & Barry Jones

HarperCollins*Publishers*

Acknowledgement

Our sincere thanks to Ray Powell for the privilege of featuring some of the magnificent crystals from his very special private collection.

HarperCollinsPublishers

First published in Australia in 1996
by HarperCollins*Publishers* Pty Limited

ACN 009 913 517
A member of the HarperCollins*Publishers* (Australia) Pty Limited Group

HarperCollins*Publishers*
25 Ryde Road, Pymble, Sydney NSW 2073, Australia
31 View Road, Glenfield, Auckland 10, New Zealand
77–85 Fulham Palace Road, London W6 8JB, United Kingdom
Hazelton Lanes, 55 Avenue Road, Suite 2900, Toronto, Ontario M5R 3L2
and 1995 Markham Road, Scarborough, Ontario M1B 5M8, Canada
10 East 53rd Street, New York NY 10032, USA

National Library of Australia Cataloguing-in-Publication data:

Jones, Wendy.
The magic of crystals: the energy and healing power of Earth's natural wonders
Includes index.

ISBN 0 7322 5714 - X.
1.Crystals - therapeutic use. 2.New Age movement. 3.Crystals - Miscellanea.
I.Jones, Barry, 1960-.
II.Title.
133.322

Illustrations on pages 38-39, 74-75 and 105 by Karen Carter
All other illustrations by Russell Jeffery
Photographs by Louise Lister

Printed in Hong Kong

9 8 7 6 5 4 3 2 1
00 99 98 97 96

Dedication

In memory of our father, Jonah Jones (1913-1973), for teaching us always to look beyond that which we see.

Contents

CHAPTER ONE

The World Beneath Our Feet

No matter where life's journey takes you,
   you are loved, you are unique.
Tread softly on the pathway
   there are jewels beneath your feet.

The Earth Story

Crystals occur in a myriad of colours, shapes and sizes. Some can be quite plain and uninteresting in appearance whilst others can be exquisitely breathtaking. Whatever the shape, colour, size or value of a stone, each is spectacular in its own right. When we look at crystals we are truly looking at the Earth's natural wonders.

To understand crystals we must go back to the beginning, to the creation of the Universe some 10,000 million years ago when all matter and energy were massed together in space. An explosion of astronomical proportions sent everything hurtling outwards in the form of a dense gas on an incredible journey to form our continually expanding Universe. As the gas formed galaxies of stars, some of the

Western Australian tiger iron with African tiger eye, pink and green tourmaline (Brazil), boulder opal (Australia), azurite and calcite (USA)

fiery fragments came together to form our sun. During the next 5,000 million years, as the sun continued its journey it drew into its orbit a gigantic cloud of gas and dust particles. As this cloud revolved, trapped for ever in the sun's orbit, swirls and eddies appeared and they formed the nuclei of the planets of our solar system. The planet Earth was born.

Earth is one of the nine planets in our solar system and is the third nearest to the sun. It consists of three different layers — the crust, the mantle and the core. The diameter of the Earth is nearly 13,000 kilometres (8,077 miles); however, the crust — where crystals and gemstones are found — varies from 6 kilometres (4 miles) under the oceans to 65 kilometres (40 miles) under mountain ranges. It is made of an upper granite zone and a lower basalt zone. The layer under the crust is formed of denser rock called the mantle and extends down some 3,000 kilometres (1,864 miles). At the centre of the Earth is the core which is thought to be composed of molten iron.

The Rock Story

The Earth is built of rocks — the rugged mountain peaks to the golden grains of sand on the beach are all rock. These rocks can be divided into three groups.

Igneous Rocks

Igneous rocks were once magma (molten rock). There are two types of igneous rock: the coarse-grained granites which form when magma from the upper part of the mantle migrates upwards through the crust and cools below the surface of the Earth, and the finer-grained basalts which are ejected from erupting volcanoes in the form of lava.

Sedimentary Rocks

Sedimentary rocks are formed by the accumulation of material caused by activity upon the surface of the Earth's crust. Most sedimentary rocks are formed under the sea. Some are created by weathering and erosion and carried by rivers, waves and winds.

Metamorphic Rocks

These are either igneous or sedimentary rocks that have undergone a mineral or structural change from heat, pressure or chemical changes in the Earth's crust.

The Mineral Story

The rocks that form the Earth are made up of minerals. In fact, most rocks are made up of a number of different minerals. Most minerals occur in the crystal form, though not all minerals grow crystals. The majority of minerals are formed deep, deep down in the Earth, and (with the exception of mercury) are solid substances made up of atoms. Each mineral has a unique chemical composition and character which remains the same wherever that mineral is found.

Crystals are minerals which display a regular external geometric shape in the form of plane faces, angles and edges. No matter how distorted that external shape is, the crystal's internal atomic structure is always the same.

Some minerals do not possess a regular geometric shape and the internal atomic structure is not always orderly. These minerals are called *amorphous*.

Minerals that outwardly resemble amorphous substances yet internally have the regimented crystal structure are called *cryptocrystalline*.

Gems which are derived from animals and plants are called organic. They include amber — the fossilised resin of coniferous trees, coral — calcified formations created by marine polyps, jet — a bituminous coal which is the fossilised remains of trees, and pearl — produced by molluscs. (In gemmological terms ivory is also included. However, out of respect to the animals who are endangered and slaughtered in the collection of ivory we choose not to include it in our book.)

The Crystal Systems

One of the most amazing aspects of crystals is that the outward geometric shape always occurs no matter how out of shape the crystal appears. This is called crystal symmetry and it is according to the elements of symmetry that crystals are divided into different systems. Symmetry can be defined in three ways: the plane of symmetry, the axis of symmetry and the centre of symmetry.

Firstly, the *plane of symmetry*, when the crystal can be divided into identical halves, as in mirror reflections of each other.

Secondly, the *axis of symmetry* — an imaginary line passing through the centre of the crystal. If the crystal is rotated 360 degrees about this line the number of times an identical face appears denotes the different axes of the crystal.

Lastly, the *centre of symmetry*, when a crystal has at least two faces parallel to each other which lie on opposite sides of the crystal.

There are thirty-two crystal classes defined by the above elements of symmetry and these are divided into seven systems. Each system has different crystal axes and different angles at which these axes intersect. Within each system many different shapes and forms can occur; however, all are related to the shape of their original crystal system. These are the seven systems:

Cubic (Isometric) System

The crystals in this system are essentially cube-shaped (as illustrated below) with three pairs of faces all the same size and at right angles to each other. Typical shapes are the octahedron (eight-sided figure) and the rhombic dodecahedron (twelve-sided figure). They include such notables as diamond, fluorite, garnet, gold and silver.

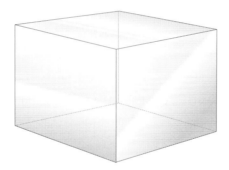

Tetragonal System

This form is an elongated cube having three pairs of faces at right angles to each other, but only two pairs of faces the same size. Typical crystal forms in this system are the tetragonal prism (as illustrated above right) and dipyramid (resembling two pyramids with the bases joined together). This system includes apophyllite, rutile and zircon.

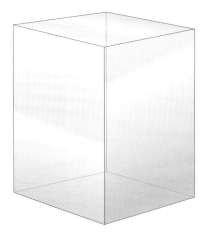

Hexagonal System

This system is often grouped together with the trigonal system because of their similar shape. The form is a six-sided figure with the sides of equal width. Typical crystal shapes in this system are the hexagonal prism (as illustrated below) and the hexagonal dipyramid (which resembles two six-sided pyramids joined together at the bases). Crystals in this system include apatite, aquamarine and emerald.

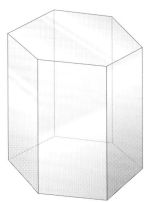

Trigonal System

Often considered a sub-system of the hexagonal. The form is like the hexagonal (six-sided), but with the sides differing in symmetry. Typical crystal shapes in this system are the trigonal prism (as illustrated below) and the dipyramid. This system includes agate, amethyst, clear quartz, tiger eye and tourmaline.

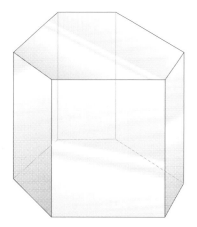

Orthorhombic System

This form is matchbox-shaped with three unequal pairs of faces at right angles to each other. Typical crystal shapes in this system are the prism (as illustrated above right) and the dipyramid. Crystals in this system include celestite, peridot and topaz.

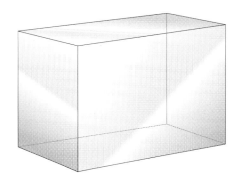

Monoclinic System

In this system no pairs of faces are the same, two pairs are at right angles to each other, and the third pair is inclined. Typical crystal shapes in this system are prisms with inclined faces (as illustrated below). This system includes azurite, malachite and moonstone.

Triclinic System

The least symmetrical of the systems, no pairs of faces are at right angles to, or of the same dimensions as each other. Typical crystal shapes in this system are the prism (as illustrated below) and the dipyramid. This system includes amazonite, rhodonite and turquoise.

On paper, the different systems are easy to identify but, as with many things, they are not quite so easy to distinguish in real life. Consider the following aspects of crystallography and then look closely at a clear quartz cluster. You will see that each individual crystal is different, yet every one will have six faces and an identical internal structure. The term applied to this assemblage of faces is crystal *form* — that is, the overall shape of the crystal. Not all crystals are as easy to observe as a clear quartz cluster, though. Consider a piece of agate — its appearance is totally different because the individual crystals cannot be seen, yet it is classified under the same crystal system. This is because it is cryptocrystalline; its form is externally different but its internal structure is the same as that of clear quartz.

The shape that crystals take is called the crystal *habit*. This can vary widely — some crystals are so tiny they look like individual hairs, some grow tightly massed together, and some resemble the petals of a flower or balls of cotton.

Most minerals tend to grow grouped together, often not showing the crystal faces. These are called *aggregates*.

Some crystals grow as *twins*: this phenomenon occurs during crystallisation when they form in such a way that they are joined at a crystallographic plane.

Crystals can also enclose other substances. These are termed *inclusions*. This occurs when another mineral or liquid is enveloped by the crystal during its growth. A good example of this is the green chlorite that can sometimes be found in clear quartz.

Crystallography, the science of crystals, is fascinating and spell-binding, an enchanting world of intricate forms, amazing patterns and spectacular shapes.

CHAPTER TWO

From Stone Age to New Age

Down through the mists of time people have collected and used gems and crystals. They have been used for adornment and talismans, tools and weapons, for foretelling the future, as amulets against evil, for barter and trading and for healing. Philosophies have been built around them, battles have been fought over them, economies have been built upon them. The allure that they possess cannot be denied.

Ritual and Religion

The use of stones in religious ceremonies in all cultures can be traced back through antiquity. Stones have been used to adorn the statues and images of gods and goddesses. Images have been carved from stone and tablets of stone engraved with sacred writings. If we look at modern-day religion we can still see the collection, use and reverence of these stones.

The ancient Egyptians carved their sacred scripture on the stone tablets and gemstones which were used in their burial ceremonies. Some precious stones, especially diamonds, were considered sacred

Hand-made crystal jewellery from Brazil, clear quartz cluster (USA), flower amethyst (Brazil), clear quartz sphere (Switzerland), faceted topaz and peridot (Australia), faceted citrine and amethyst (Brazil)

in the Hindu culture and stories tell of the fabulous Kalpa Tree, a symbolic offering to the gods, which is described by Hindu poets as being fashioned from a glowing mass of stones, with roots of sapphire, a trunk of diamond, cat's eye and topaz and foliage of zircon and coral. Pearls and emeralds hung from its boughs and its fruits were rubies. Gemstones and jewellery are still deemed to be worthy offerings in the Hindu faith, the belief being that such an offering will bring good luck.

Crystals and gemstones were frequently mentioned in the Bible. The Book of Exodus in the Old Testament tells of God appearing to Moses standing on a pavement of sapphire. It also describes in detail the breastplate of the High-priest of Israel set with twelve stones, each representing one of the twelve tribes of Israel. These stones are said to have been sardius, topaz, carbuncle, emerald, sapphire, diamond, jacinth, agate, amethyst, beryl, onyx and jasper. The Book of Revelation in the New Testament describes how the walls of the new Jerusalem were made of jasper and the foundations adorned with many precious stones.

In Peru at the time of the Spanish Conquest there existed a huge emerald which was believed to be the goddess Umina who was held in great awe. The priests exhibited the stone on holy days and the local people who flocked to visit the shrine were encouraged to bring emeralds as offerings as the stones were deemed to be the daughters of the goddess.

In the Aztec culture in Mexico turquoise was considered to be a stone of the gods. No-one was allowed to wear or own it as turquoise was used exclusively as an offering in the temple or as a decoration on sacred images.

In North America legend has it that turquoise and red coral necklaces were worn by the four Navajo rain gods. Thus a piece of turquoise, thrown into the river as a prayer for rain was recited, was said to ensure that rain would fall. A number of Native American tribes considered turquoise to be sacred. Pieces of turquoise, beads and jewellery — often in great numbers — have been found in the burial mounds of the Pueblo tribes. Turquoise has also been found in burial sites in many countries in South America. The close association with turquoise lives on to the present day.

Staurolite is a crystal twin that forms in the shape of a cross. It is a stone that was once called *lapis crucifer* ('stone cross') and is often referred to today as a fairy cross or fairy stone. The story is that it is the tears of the fairies who, when told of the crucifixion of Jesus Christ, cried with such anguish that their teardrops crystallised into tiny crosses.

In thirteenth-century Italy the diamond — *amante di Dio*, ('lover of

Silver chalice set with turquoise, pearl, emerald, carnelian and solid gold scarab; silver dagger made from 2.5 kg (5¹/₂ lb) silver with a 132-carat star quartz crystal set into the top of the handle which is encrusted with 30 faceted amethysts and moonstone and star quartz cabochons; Trobriand cross set with natural pearls and faceted amethyst; silver and enamel box with carved tiger eye stone set on lid

God') was revered as a sacred stone to be used for religious purposes.

Clear quartz symbolised the purity of heart and spirit of those within the Church.

Amulets and Talismans

Throughout history, and in all cultures, amulets and talismans have been and still are used. An amulet is a defence, a charm of protection, worn to ward off evil and bad luck. A talisman is used to attract health, success and happiness — it is a good luck charm. Amulets and talismans come in many forms from feathers, seeds and plants to sacred writings and symbols and they often involve much ritual and magic. Crystals, rocks and gems have always been a major component of many of these charms.

The ancient Egyptians engraved amulets of stone with text from the Book of the Dead, which contained spells and rituals to help the deceased through to the afterlife. These engravings, on carnelian, lapis lazuli, jasper and other stones, were placed upon the bodies of the dead to ensure protection and safe passage for the soul. One amulet considered to possess great power was that of an eye fashioned from lapis lazuli or turquoise and gold to ward off evil. That amulet is still worn today in some Middle Eastern countries.

In the tomb of Tutankhamun 143 amulets and pieces of jewellery made of gold, lapis lazuli, turquoise, carnelian, clear quartz, jasper, obsidian, amazonite and jade were discovered.

* Amethyst was worn by soldiers who believed it would protect them in battle. (It was also carried as an antidote to drunkenness!)
* Aquamarine was a talisman carried by sailors to give them courage and to protect them from the perils of the sea.
* Banded agate was in huge demand in the middle of the last century in Sudan. The white bands on the brown and black agate symbolised the eye and were thought to protect the wearer against the 'evil eye'.
* Diamonds were considered lucky both in India and ancient Rome. The Hindus divided diamonds into four different categories according to the major castes. Each category brought different things to the owner of the diamond — to the Brahmin it brought power, friendship and wealth, to the Kshatriya eternal youth, to the Vaisya success and to the Sudra good fortune. Romans wore uncut diamonds set in gold rings as talismans. Napoleon carried a sword set with a diamond into battle as the stone was said to make the owner unconquerable.

* Emerald was worn as an amulet against epilepsy and fever. It was also revered as it was said to allow the wearer to see into the future.

* Jade was considered a most powerful amulet in ancient China because it was thought to have the power to give and preserve life. The New Zealand Maoris also valued jade as a talisman of great power and carved *hei-tiki* (meaning 'a carved image for the neck') pendants from this material featuring images of long-dead ancestors. These were passed down from generation to generation and it was considered that the wearing of the *hei-tiki* actually communicated part of the very being of these ancestors to the wearer.

* Moonstone was held to be a sacred stone in India and was often given as a talisman to brides and grooms, as it was believed to arouse tender passions.

* Opal was the talisman of thieves and spies as it was said to make the wearer invisible!

* Peridot was carried as an amulet to ward off evil spirits.

* Rubies were worn through the ages as amulets of great power. The Burmese even inserted rubies into their flesh in the belief that they could make them invincible. It was believed that a ruby could warn the wearer of danger by becoming dark

and dull. Catherine of Aragon, the first wife of Henry VIII, predicted her own downfall from the darkening of her ruby ring.

✳ Sapphires were said to banish fraud and were carried by the French in the thirteenth century to ward off poverty.

✳ Turquoise was carried for luck in both India and Persia, for it was believed in both cultures that if you were to see the reflection of the new moon in a piece of turquoise good luck and protection were assured. In Persia turquoise was also attached to horses to protect the rider from falling. And in North America Apache warriors would tie pieces of turquoise to their bows to ensure accurate aim. Indeed, turquoise was so highly prized for its talismanic qualities that for a medicine man not to have had turquoise stones in his possession would have dramatically lessened his standing in the tribe.

✳ Zircon was used as an amulet by travellers to protect against accident and injury on the journey. It was also used to stop the wearer from being struck by lightening.

As we look back through history the list of stones used as amulets and talismans is long. However, there is one stone that stands out from the rest — a stone that appears universally across many cultures, from Eskimos at the top of the world to North American Cherokees, to the shamans of Malaysia and South America — a stone of great magic, of power and light. That stone is clear quartz.

Potions and Lotions

The emergence of crystals in healing is not a new phenomenon. The laying-on of stones is a very ancient art and nowadays more and more people are rediscovering the wonders of crystal healing.

In the past, crystals and stones were often used medicinally. Elixirs and potions were made from stones steeped in liquid or crushed into grains or powder.

* Amber was made into an ointment and used to treat coughs and bronchitis.
* Agate was ground and mixed with wine to heal wounds.
* Aquamarine was prescribed as a cure for toothache, epilepsy and liver disease.
* Emerald was taken as an antidote to poison and to stop dysentery.
* Bloodstone was used to stop haemorrhaging.
* Diamonds were not always used beneficially: they were long thought to be poisonous and diamond dust was used to this end.

* Hematite was favoured in ancient Egypt to stop heavy bleeding and reduce swelling.
* Jade was widely used by the Chinese to strengthen the heart and lungs and prolong life. Mixed with rice and dew, it was taken to strengthen the muscles and harden bones.
* Lapis lazuli has been used since the time of the ancient Egyptians where it was used in the making of eye ointments. It was used by the Greeks as an antidote to snakebite and later as a cure for fever and depression.
* Sapphires were used in the treatment of eye diseases and the plague.
* Topaz was steeped in wine for three days and then rubbed across the eyes to cure poor vision.

Crystals have also been used as colouring agents. In ancient Egypt, lapis lazuli was ground into a fine powder and used as eye make-up.

In medieval times wonderful illuminated manuscripts were written. The meticulously hand-scripted pages were embellished with brilliantly coloured decorations and pictures. These paints were derived from nature. Reds, yellows and browns from ochre, blue from powdered lapis lazuli and azurite and green from malachite. Gold was hammered into leaves as fine as cobwebs.

The healing powers of crystals and minerals appear to have been universal. There is much lore and legend involved, some humorous, some absurd and some which today would be considered lethal! However, out of this mythology a truth is shining as brightly as any gemstone. That truth is that there is an energy within the stones that has the power to heal. Healing happens on many levels and is not just restricted to the physical. The dedicated crystal healers of today are working with tools that have been used for thousands of years. Many 'alternative' healing practices are now becoming widely accepted as we open our minds to a new age of healing and learning. With that healing and learning comes a respect and understanding for all that exists.

Rings and Things

The need to adorn our bodies with ornaments appears in nearly every culture. From the time when people first adorned themselves with feathers, shells and pebbles, the fascination with the wearing of crystals and gems has never ceased. Modern-day jewellery could well be considered plain when we look at what some of our ancestors wore. Crystals and gems have been crafted into every conceivable type of adornment from crowns and tiaras to bracelets and rings, from belts and buckles to nose rings and anklets. Indeed, many people don't feel 'dressed' without jewellery. And have you ever noticed how costume jewellery just doesn't feel 'right'? Is this merely habit or an unrecognised need to feel surrounded by the energies only genuine gems can impart?

Down through the ages certain gemstones have been prized above all others. The diamond stands alone — it is the hardest, and therefore the most durable, of all stones, and manifests a brilliance that is unique. The ruby, sapphire and emerald share this gemstone's throne as they do in the crowns and sceptres of the royal houses of the world.

Much has been written of the fabulous gems of the world. The Koh-i-Noor diamond, the Star of India sapphire, the Black Prince's ruby ... the list is long and priceless. But is our lifelong fascination with these stones merely to do with their rarity and value, or is it something more? Everyone knows that diamonds aren't a girl's best friend any more, yet we still strive to have this sparkling gem on our finger. Is it perhaps that, as well as its beauty, we need the diamond's energies, brilliance and purity in our life?

In recent times more and more people are putting aside their traditional jewels. Amethyst and clear quartz, for example, are being worn in place of more highly valued stones. Often gold is being replaced by silver, perhaps because silver's energies seem to blend more harmoniously with such stones. Is this a passing fad? We think not, believing that more and more people will be drawn to the wearing of stones that they instinctively feel they need in their lives rather than the dictates of fashion or status.

Atlantis

This fabulous lost city has captured and inspired the imagination since the time of Ancient Greece. It is said that some 10,000 years BC there existed in the Atlantic Ocean, beyond the Straits of Gibraltar, a vast island continent ruled by a mighty empire. It was believed to be an advanced civilisation that flourished and prospered until a time came when — some say by earthquake, others by a catastrophe caused by humans — Atlantis sank and was lost for ever beneath the sea.

Since the time of the first stories of Atlantis, by Plato, much has been written about this lost city and many different theories have been put forward as to its origin, whereabouts and demise. Much of the information regarding Atlantis is thought to have been channelled from higher beings. Some say that the original Atlantians came from another planet bringing with them an advanced technology. Whatever its origins, it is said that the city's technology was built on the science of crystals — a science that was lost when Atlantis disappeared. There are many references to the use of crystals in the stories about Atlantis and many detailed descriptions of the crystal healing techniques that were used. It is believed that the wisdom and knowledge of the Atlantians have been stored inside certain crystals and that when the time is right these crystals will surface into the world. Many people believe that the healing work that is being done on the Earth today is preparing for that time.

Places of Power

Throughout the world there are natural places of power, places where the Earth's energies are so strong that to feel their influence will be an experience that will remain with you for ever.

Two much-visited and much-talked-about places are Uluru (Ayers Rock) in central Australia and Sedona in northern Arizona, USA. The pilgrimage of visitors today to these remote areas of the world is nothing new. The Australian Aborigine and the Native American have always recognised this Earth power and these places were held to be most sacred. To stand beneath the awe-inspiring Uluru is truly to glimpse the power and vastness of the Earth. The energies of the vortexes in the red rocks of Sedona reach to the very centre of your being. Once touched you know, just as the Native Americans knew, that you will be drawn to return. Wherever you are it is possible to discover and tune into these energies.

Circles and Stones

There are also places of power throughout the world which in ancient times people marked out as sacred sites. Stonehenge in Great Britain is probably the most famous of all the stone megalith circles and conjures up wonderful images of druids and pagan rituals.

Interestingly, the majority of these standing stones appear to have been chosen for their very high content of quartz crystal. The Duloe Circle in Cornwall in England is comprised entirely of megaliths of white quartz; every stone in the Callanish Circle on the Isle of Lewis off the Scottish coast contains white quartz or feldspar; and the inner ring of some Welsh circles were paved with quartz. So quartz crystal obviously played a vital role in the use of these circles. Was it because crystals and crystalline stones were used to store the energy that was generated in the circle, for use at a later time? Were they used to transmit that energy at the time, or — as is more likely — as a protective shield against outside energies entering the circle?

Research has been carried out at some of these sites, notably at the Rollright Stones in Oxfordshire, England, which were the subject of the Dragon Project, set up in 1978 to investigate the energies at these ancient sites and the ley lines that join them. The fascinating findings concerning the energies in the circles are still the basis of ongoing investigation today.

Circles have been used in many cultures from the ancient standing stones in the British Isles to the Native American medicine wheel and the Chinese Feng Shui compass. As children we are taught to hold hands and form a circle. It is yet another linking of energies.

The Age of Aquarius

The interest in crystals in the New Age is not a new discovery, rather, it is an awakening, a rediscovery of the Earth and the Earth energies and the realisation of who we are and how precious those energies are to us. Much of what we are now learning our ancestors knew and practised throughout their lives.

As the planets revolve around the sun, the sun travels a path through the twelve zodiac constellations. This path is in the opposite direction to the journey of the planets through the constellations. The sun remains in each constellation for approximately 2,100 years. About 4,000 BC the sun was in the constellation of Taurus and about 2,000 BC entered the Age of Aries.

The Piscean Age heralded an age of great change. The astronomers and priests foretold of the age of iron — a masculine age when the sun would dominate the moon. So it has been. Somehow the age of technology engulfed our original Earth wisdom and for a time it was

40

swept away. During that time much harm has been done to the Earth. The ravages of war and disease, the wilful destruction of Earth and Her creatures and the growing violence in our societies have brought us to a point where the future could look black indeed.

We are now standing at the dawn of the Aquarian Age. The new golden age, an age of harmony, understanding and spiritual growth. There is an anticipation and excitement heralding this age of peace, for soon the aggressions of the Piscean Age will be behind us. It is not too late to mend the wrongs of our recent past. Every day more people are embracing the New Age philosophy, rediscovering the Earth energies and playing their own important part in the healing of this planet. The crystals have chosen this time to resurface in our memories to be used as guides and tools as we step forward into the next millennium.

CHAPTER THREE

The Crystal Story

You are born of the Earth with the wisdom of the stars.
White light keeper, you are friend and teacher.
You are clear quartz.

Clear Quartz

This is the stone that most people recognise or visualise as crystal.
The word 'crystal' comes from the Greek word *krustallos* meaning
'ice'. It was once believed that clear quartz crystals were comprised
of water that had been eternally frozen. Clear, or rock crystal, as it is
also known, is found in many parts of the world; however, the main
sources are in Brazil in South America and Arkansas in North
America. Clear quartz is comprised of silicon dioxide and forms in
the trigonal system as hexagonal prisms. It is mainly transparent and
colourless but is often white and cloudy, especially near the base.
Every crystal is unique, so the size and shape can vary considerably.
Most crystals will show inclusions in the form of swirls and feathers
often resembling amazing intricate 'galaxies'.

Clear quartz is known as the energy stone because of its unique
ability to absorb, store, amplify and transmit energy. From crystal

Spectacular faceted citrine from Brazil 200 mm (8 in) tall and weighing over
8,000 carats. The next largest citrine pictured weighs 624 carats

radio sets to quartz watches, it is a tiny piece of quartz crystal that makes these inventions work. Quartz crystal has piezoelectric properties; that is, when pressure or heat is applied to a quartz crystal the energy stored in the crystal is transformed into electricity. This property makes clear quartz one of the most important crystals.

Clear quartz appears in a number of different forms.

Clear Quartz Clusters

These are formations of single-terminated crystals that share a common base. Clusters can vary in size from a few millimetres to huge formations weighing up to several tons and may comprise of several or several hundred individual crystal points. Clear quartz clusters are both fascinating and very beautiful pieces to own. The energies of this crystal will uplift and harmonise any area or room.

Generator Crystals

Generator crystals are single quartz crystals in which the six faces join sharply together to form the terminated apex (tip). The energy of the crystal flows from that point. They are naturally occurring but can also be bought cut and polished to that shape (every face and side will be polished and the base cut straight so the crystal can stand). Sizes can range from about a centimetre (⅖ inch) upwards. Generator crystals are powerful crystal pieces that are ideal to use in meditation and chakra work. Small generator crystals are excellent to use as pendulums.

Double-terminated Crystals

Naturally occurring shapes that have formed with an apex at either end. The energy in these crystals can flow either or both ways. Many crystals used in jewellery are fashioned into this shape and it remains one of the most popular stone cuts.

Phantom Crystals

These are rare and fascinating crystals. If when you look into a crystal you see the 'ghost' of a crystal shape inside it, you will know that you are lucky enough to possess a phantom crystal. Sometimes this ghost will be very faint, sometimes it may be quite distinct with an almost solid colour. Phantom crystals show that the crystal has grown and stopped and continued on through many lifetimes of learning.

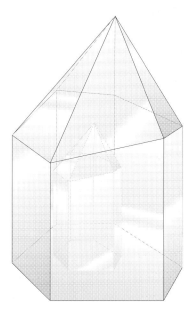

Phantom crystals are wonderful to use and carry, though they should be treated with much respect for they are powerful tools. They can be used as a focus in meditation to access past lives and the higher self.

Laser Wands

Some people are disappointed when they first see a laser wand as they are not as spectacular as many of the other crystal forms. Laser wands have etched markings and lines upon them and can be quite dull and rugged in appearance. Long, slender, finger-like crystals with small faces comprise the termination. It is said that laser wands were used in the healing temples of Lemuria, a fabled empire which is said to have existed prior to Atlantis (and is considered by some to be Australia). These crystals are called 'psychic scalpels' and can be used to perform psychic 'surgery'. They should be treated with the highest respect and used with great care.

A laser wand can also be used to create a protective barrier by using it to draw an energy circle around yourself or an object. This energy field can be so strong that it renders the subject 'invisible'. When doing this, never point the wand at another person as it is capable of cutting through the auric field.

Channelling Crystals

A crystal with a large seven-sided face at the front and a perfect triangle face at the back. These crystals should be used with great care. They are excellent for meditation and for seeking inner guidance (see Chapter 4).

Rainbow Crystals

As children, we want to find the end of the rainbow; as adults, we recognise the amazing beauty of the phenomenon. The seven colours — red, orange, yellow, green, blue, indigo and violet — that form the rainbow spectrum appear when white light is refracted. We normally only see these colours refracted through lead crystal (see Chapter 4) or as an arc across the sky during a rainstorm.

However, on rare occasions, crystals can be found that actually contain rainbows. This is due to the internal fractures in some stones which refract the light, thus causing a rainbow to appear, captured inside the crystal. These magical crystals are uplifting and inspiring and are wonderful to use for meditation. Rainbows can also be found in other crystals but their appearance is usually more spectacular in clear quartz. If you find a rainbow crystal you will treasure it for ever.

Window Crystals

Window crystals have a large diamond-shaped face at the front of the crystal. The point at the top of the diamond connects to a line leading to the apex of the crystal; the side points connect to the angles of the adjoining faces. The bottom point of the diamond connects to a line running to the base. The window face is large enough to be considered a seventh face. Many crystals display a small diamond, but these are not window crystals.

Window crystals are to use only on the self; they reflect the true identity of the user. Only when you are ready to look into your own soul and accept the truth will you find a window crystal.

These crystals can be used in meditation by gazing into the window or by holding the window to the third eye (a point in the middle of the forehead which we use to look beyond the Earth plane).

48

Tabular Crystals

Frequently double-terminated, tabular, or 'tabby' crystals have two flat, wide, opposing sides which often have ridged markings. They are used to link and activate other crystals and can be used as a bridge between different levels of awareness.

Sceptre Crystals

Aptly named and easily recognisable, sceptre crystals look as if a crystal rod has been inserted into the base of the crystal. The crystal has in fact grown around the rod to create this regal formation. It is said that these crystals were carried by the high priests and priestesses of Atlantis and Lemuria. These beautiful formations can also occur in other types of quartz crystal.

Record-keeper Crystals

One or more small triangles are etched into one of the faces of this crystal, but you could search for your whole life and never find one of these precious pieces. Record-keeper crystals are rare indeed and are not something that you can buy. They are sacred crystals in which ancient knowledge and wisdom is stored. It is said that they were programmed by the Atlantians and Lemurians to save and store their ancient knowledge until the time came when they could release that knowledge back into the world. If you are meant to be a temporary custodian of a record-keeper crystal it will come into your life. If this happens to you, it is a very special honour.

Elestial Crystals

These unique crystals look very different to other crystals and can be recognised by the many etched markings and natural terminations that form all over the body of the stone. They are very special crystals that carry with them memories of the time before humankind existed. As powerful meditation pieces they can assist us in our understanding of the life and death experience, help us to overcome our emotional problems and are channels for exploring our spirituality.

Amethyst, Citrine, Rose Quartz and Smoky Quartz

Amethyst

More people seem drawn to amethyst than any other semi-precious stone. This is hardly surprising as in today's hectic, fast-moving and often noisy world the calming peaceful vibrations of amethyst reach out to sooth and relax.

Amethyst is found in various locations throughout the world but the most spectacular and sought-after stone is found in the state of Minas Gerais in Brazil.

Amethyst is the most highly valued stone in the quartz family.

It takes its colour — which can range from the palest lilac to the deepest purple — from trace amounts of ferric iron in the quartz. Amethyst forms in the trigonal system as hexagonal prisms. Unlike clear quartz, the individual points do not grow to any great length and often the deepest colour appears at the point and fades away towards the base. Some amethyst geodes are so large that when cut in half they form a crystal cave large enough to stand in! The word 'amethyst' comes from the Greek *amethustos*, meaning 'to push away drunkenness'.

Amethyst is often called the peace stone. It is a good stone for meditation and spirituality, reflecting the colour of the seventh ray — violet. Amethyst meditations can be quite special and very purifying. Amethyst can be used to open the crown chakra and increase your levels of awareness and understanding as well as increasing psychic and channelling abilities.

Amethyst also makes an excellent bedside rock — the calming qualities of the stone make it the perfect night-time companion to relax the body and mind and encourage deep restful sleep. It can also be used to cure headaches and migraines and can be of particular comfort during periods of great sadness, stress or bereavement.

Amethyst has particularly strong protective qualities. Many people choose to wear amethyst jewellery or carry a small piece with them.

Citrine

Natural citrine takes its name from its lemony colour which can vary from a light champagne to cognac. It forms in the trigonal system as hexagonal prisms on a common base. Naturally occurring citrine is rare and in fact most citrine sold today is amethyst which has been heat-treated. This process turns the amethyst bright to deep orange-gold. There are small deposits of citrine in a number of countries although most of the heated citrine comes from Brazil.

You will find citrine an important part of your crystal collection. With its appearance of having captured the sun, citrine really is the stone of joy. Citrine is a stone of plenty which attracts abundance on all levels, and it is useful to have around you in business. The energies of citrine are warm and uplifting and it helps to stimulate mental focus to higher levels.

Whilst many people prefer to use natural citrine because it is not contrived, do not dismiss heat-treated stones. Rely on your intuition when making your selection.

Rose Quartz

Rose quartz forms in the trigonal system in massive form as compact prisms. It forms infrequently as a developed crystal structure, but these beautiful pieces are a rare find. The stone takes its name from its colour, which ranges from pale to deep pink. It is found in a number of different places, but Brazil is the major source.

Rose quartz is known as the love stone. Indeed, its very appearance justifies its name — it truly is a stone of the heart. Rose quartz works on the emotions, balancing and harmonising. It is the perfect stone for those who feel unloved, and its gentle calming influences go towards healing emotional wounds. In times of emotional turmoil wearing a rose quartz pendant on a chain over your heart chakra can be a great help.

So often we carry the jealousies and frustrations we feel with us instead of letting go and releasing. The soothing influences of rose quartz will work on those pent-up emotions as you sleep. It would make a good bedside rock next to your amethyst as the two stones harmonise well together.

Rose quartz is a beautiful gift to give to someone you love and can be especially helpful to young teenagers as they come to terms with their awakening and changing emotions.

Smoky Quartz

The very name of this stone sounds mysterious and exotic. It is also known as smoky topaz. Its colour — which gives it its name — ranges from a very pale grey-brown to black. Smoky quartz forms in the trigonal system as hexagonal prisms and is found in numerous locations around the world. The very black stones are called morion. Be aware that there are heat-treated smokys on the market today which are hard to distinguish from the morion. The shop keeper should be able to tell you if the stone is natural, but if in doubt rely upon your intuition.

Smoky quartz is recommended for grounding and balancing, having strong protective qualities. It is a good stone to carry with you after any higher-state meditations to reaffirm your links with the Earth.

Smoky quartz is unique in that it can actually absorb and dissolve negative energies by clearing away emotional blockages and thus allowing positive energies to take their place. It is a positive stone to use in channelling work. If you work with computers it is a good idea to place a piece of smoky quartz between you and the computer, to absorb any rays that may be given off by the machine.

Other Important Stones

Agate

A variety of chalcedony which often shows bands and patterns, agate is named after the Achates River in Sicily. It forms in the trigonal system as microcrystalline nodules and geodes. Agate occurs in many parts of the world in various beautiful natural colours. Examples include blue lace agate — very pale blue with white lacy markings; Mexican crazy lace agate — delightful paisley-pattern marking, can be a wonderful pinky-red and white, sometimes yellow, grey and white; moss agate — colourless, with green, moss-like inclusions.

Agate is known as the strength stone: it imparts a sense of this quality both mentally and physically. It also balances and grounds on all levels. Recently, banded agate has been dyed on a large scale and is now popular as bookends, figurines and polished shapes. Some of these dyed pieces can be quite spectacular as the banding on the stone absorbs different degrees of colour. Blues, greens, reds and recently purple and pink are now available.

*A*mazonite

An inspiring stone reflecting the colours of the sky and the ocean. Amazonite is a type of feldspar which takes its name from the Amazon. It does, however, also occur in other parts of the world. Sometimes called Amazon stone, it forms in the triclinic system as prismatic crystals in the most beautiful turquoise-blue colour.

Amazonite is a lovely stone to wear in jewellery around the neck because it is one of the stones that works well with the throat chakra. It aligns and balances both the mental and physical bodies. As well, it has a great calming influence and stimulates creativity and communication, and understanding of the self.

Amber

Amber brings golden light into our lives, capturing not only the colours of the sun but our imagination as well. It is the fossilised resin of coniferous trees dating back many millions of years ago. Our fascination with amber dates back to prehistoric times. In recent years interest in amber skyrocketed with the release of the book and film *Jurassic Park*, the fictional story of recreating dinosaurs by using the blood from mosquitoes fossilised in amber. The main source of amber is the Baltic and it ranges in colour from pale yellow to golden-brown. Insects, leaves, flowers and seeds are often found suspended in time inside amber nodules. Amber has a stabilising effect and can absorb negativity and in doing this allows the body to heal itself.

Aquamarine

One of the most beautiful of stones, its name translates as 'water of the sea' and it was believed that wearing aquamarine would give protection on sea voyages. It is easy to understand its association with the sea for the colours of the ocean are truly captured within this stone. Aquamarine is a variety of beryl which forms in the hexagonal system as long prisms. The colours range from light blue to deep blue-green. Whilst occurring in a number of different parts of the world, the most important deposits are to be found in Brazil. Good-quality aquamarine suitable for faceting into gemstones has long been sought by jewellery makers.

Aquamarine is a beautiful stone both to wear and use. It is a very peaceful, compassionate stone, providing both emotional and intellectual stability and clarity of mind. It can help you become more tolerant of circumstances and take responsibility for your own actions. Good for relationships, as it symbolises hope and happiness.

*A*venturine

Aventurine is an attractive green stone that takes its name from the Italian words *a ventura* meaning 'by chance'. On close inspection you will see that the iridescent appearance of the stone is caused by sparkling mica crystals and hematite inclusions. It forms in the trigonal system in cryptocrystalline formations in various locations including Brazil and India.

Aventurine is a lovely stone to wear over the heart as its protective qualities will ward off anxiety and fear. It balances the male and female aspects, leading to a sense of wellbeing and decisiveness. A good stone to motivate and encourage positive attitudes.

*A*zurite

As the name suggests, this stone is the colour of azure blue. It forms in the monoclinic system as tabular crystals or masses. Azurite is found in various parts of the world with some of the finest examples coming from Namibia and France. It often grows near or with malachite and the two together form a very special partnership.

Azurite is truly a stone for both the mind and the soul. It is excellent to use for cleansing and then opening the mind to higher levels and awakening psychic abilities. The deep blue colour energises the third eye chakra and allows us to expand our vision, encouraging inspiration and creativity.

*B*loodstone *(H*eliotrope*)*

A dark green chalcedony with red spots, hence the commonly used name, bloodstone. Its other name, heliotrope, comes from the Greek *helios*, 'sun', and *trepein*, 'to turn'. It forms in the trigonal system in massive formations, one of the main sources being India.

Bloodstone is a strength stone and a powerful healer for both the physical and non-physical body. It is a good stone to carry when you feel stressed or off-balance. Bloodstone revitalises, renews and balances, promoting inner strength and sensitivity.

Carnelian

Carnelian is a form of chalcedony and takes its name from the Cornel cherry because of its colour, which varies from red to orange and brown. The best-quality carnelian comes from India. It forms in the trigonal system in microcrystalline formations. The colour of the stone is warming and heartening.

Carnelian is a good mind stone — it aids concentration and memory and stimulates the mind, thus dispelling apathy and mental lethargy. It encourages one to question and inquire and so is a good stone to study with.

Fluorite

Fluorite is one of the most beautiful of the New Age stones and gives its name to the word 'fluorescent'. It occurs in a variety of colours in many different regions and forms in the cubic system as masses, cubes and octahedra. It is, however, a fragile stone, so it should be handled with extra care.

Fluorite is a mind stone on all levels. It is excellent for aiding concentration and study and for advancing the mind to higher understanding. Fluorite has a strong stabilising influence and balances both positive and negative sides of the mind. It is a wonderful stone for meditation.

Garnet

When most people think of garnet they think of a red stone, but garnet actually comes in every colour except blue. It takes its name from the Latin word *granatum* meaning 'pomegranate' because of the stone's resemblance to its seedlike fruit. Other stones in the garnet family are almandine, andradite, grossular, pyrope, rhodolite, spessartine and uvarovite. Garnet forms in the cubic system as dodecahedral crystals and can be found in nearly every corner of the world.

Red garnet is a stone of the heart. It is a stone of love and compassion that balances and purifies the body's energy field. Garnet has a strong affinity with the base chakra and both balances and stimulates the kundalini (the coiled sleeping energy centred at the base chakra. The awakening and rising of the kundalini is the pathway to enlightenment). Down through the ages people have been drawn to garnet for just these reasons. Garnet makes a wonderful companion to rose quartz and the two worn together are an excellent combination.

Hematite

Hematite is one of the most important iron ores and takes its name from the Greek word *haima* meaning 'blood'. This heavy, metallic-looking dark grey stone can be polished to a mirror-like finish. It forms in the trigonal system, often as tabular (flat) crystals or masses, and is found in various parts of the world including North America and Canada.

Hematite is known as the stress stone or, to be more precise, the anti-stress stone! A piece of polished hematite makes a great pocket stone to carry in stressful situations. Hematite is also a good stone for the mind, enhancing mental capabilities and dispelling negativity. The influence of the iron has an energising effect on both the physical and non-physical bodies.

Jade

To many, jade symbolises the East. The word comes from the Spanish *piedra de ijada* meaning 'stone of the loin' and is really a misnomer. The confusion began in the sixteenth century when the name jade was given to the green stone brought back to Europe from Central and South America by the Spanish conquistadors.

In the seventeenth century the name jade was also applied to the many stone carvings arriving from China. This stone was subsequently given the name nephrite. In 1863 it was discovered that jade from the Americas and Burmese jade were different from Chinese nephrite and so the American and Burmese jades were renamed jadeite. Today, the term jade is still used to describe both stones. Jade forms in the monoclinic system, usually in masses, and occurs in many parts of the world. Precious jade is always jadeite, the most valuable of which is imperial jade from Burma.

Jade has long been worn and carried. The subtle jade energies are peaceful and nurturing. It is a good night-time stone to help in the remembering and interpretation of dreams. Jade works on the emotions, balancing and calming and encouraging wisdom and guidance.

Lapis Lazuli

Lapis lazuli takes its name from the Persian word *lazhuward* meaning 'blue'. The stone of the ancient Egyptians, lapis has long been treasured and exalted. Much used in jewellery, it is said that the golden flecks of pyrite in the deep blue stone resemble the stars in the heavens.

Lapis lazuli forms in the cubic system, mainly in masses, but can occur as cubes and dodecahedral crystals. It is actually a combination of minerals, mainly lazurite, calcite and pyrite. The two prominent sources of lapis are Chile and Afghanistan.

Lapis lazuli is a stone for the mind, to expand both the awareness and the intellect, bringing clarity and understanding. Used on the sixth chakra it can enhance psychic awareness and ability and communication with the higher self.

Malachite

Another stone that has been worn through the ages, malachite makes a beautiful partner with azurite. This magnificent vivid green stone forms in masses and needle-like crystals and can be found in many continents, the most important deposits being in Zaire. The light and dark green banding and concentric rings make malachite one of the most beautiful opaque stones. It forms in the monoclinic system in masses.

Many people are drawn to the healing colour of malachite. It is a heart stone, balancing and clarifying the emotions and clearing away subconscious and emotional blocks. It allows one to become more intuitive and understanding and to move onwards and forwards from unwanted situations. Malachite has a strong calming influence and can instil a sense of courage in times of stress.

Moonstone

Aptly named, this beautiful stone captures the aura of the moon. Moonstone ranges in colour from a milky white sheen to apricot and grey and can be found in various countries including Sri Lanka, India and Australia. It forms in the monoclinic system often as tabular crystals. Moonstone cabochons (domes) set in silver can be especially lovely to wear and it makes a wonderful partner with garnet.

*Large morion quartz from the USA, smaller smoky quartz from
Switzerland, golden sheen obsidian spheres from Mexico*

Moonstone enhances the feminine in our nature. It delicately
balances and soothes the emotions, releasing strain and tension. It
instils confidence and composure whilst encouraging a sense of
perception, intuitiveness and understanding.

Obsidian

Obsidian is Nature's glass, born out of the volcanoes. There is much
fascination today with this stone which occurs in many parts of the
world. There are a number of different types of obsidian, the most
common being black, though other colours do occur. These include
snowflake, or flowering obsidian, with white mineral inclusions
which, when polished, resemble snowflakes or flowers; mahogany
obsidian, a mottled rust-red and black; and silver sheen and golden
sheen obsidian, which are some of the most beautiful examples and
have been likened to looking at plush velvet through glass. The sheen
obsidians can be spectacular when cut into spheres, the sheen
appearing as if by magic as you turn the sphere around, and they can be
powerful pieces when used as a focus in meditation. Rainbow obsidian
exhibits beautiful iridescent bands of subtle colours. One of the most
endearing of the obsidians are the Apache tears, which are small dark
grey pebbles found in the American West. Legend says that they are the
tears of Native American women mourning their lost warriors.

Obsidian is an important New Age stone and should be used with respect. It is a grounding stone that protects and shields against negativity. Obsidian reflects your inner flaws and inadequacies and helps you to understand and correct those flaws.

Rhodonite

A beautiful pink stone with black veins which takes its name from the Greek word *rhodos* meaning 'rose-red'. Rhodonite can be found in both the Americas and in numerous locations around the world. It forms in the triclinic system, usually in masses, and on rare occasions in tabular crystal form.

Rhodonite is one of the heart stones and its loving energies inspire self-esteem and confidence. This is the stone to help you maximise your potential and give you greater understanding and discernment. Rhodonite can assist in dispelling anxiety and instils a sense of calm when facing new situations.

Sodalite

A dark blue stone interspersed with white calcite. Sodalite forms in the cubic system in masses and, very rarely, as dodecahedral crystals. It is found in numerous parts of the world including Brazil and Canada.

Sodalite is a stone that enhances communication and creative expression. It is said that the white calcite veins in the stone symbolise the ideas and inspirations breaking through. Sodalite encourages rational thinking and clarity of ideas, allowing you to recognise and accept the truth.

Tiger Eye

Tiger eye is aptly named, for its colours are truly that of a great cat's eyes. The unique yellow, gold and brown fibrous appearance of tiger eye when polished shows a wonderful lustrous velvety sheen. It forms in the trigonal system in masses and can be found in South Africa, Australia and other locations around the world. The golden energies of tiger eye bring cheerfulness and optimism. It balances the male and female aspects of the body and its soothing effects help soften stubbornness. Tiger eye is also helpful in encouraging clear and logical thinking.

Topaz

The word topaz has long been associated with the colour yellow so there is a misconception that all topaz stones are that colour. Pure topaz is in fact colourless; however, there are many colour variations — yellow, orange, red, pale blue, pink and pale green. Topaz is thought to have been named after the island of Topazos (now called Zebirget) in the Red Sea, though some say that it comes from the Sanskrit word *tapaz*, meaning 'fire'. Topaz forms in the

Green and pink tourmaline, blue topaz, aquamarine and amethyst, all from Brazil

orthorhombic system as prismatic crystals, often with terminated ends. It can be found in many parts of the world, the largest source being in Brazil.

Topaz is a wonderful stone for the self, enhancing individuality and instilling a sense of confidence and trust in one's ability. It wards off negativity, bringing a sense of joy and calmness. Topaz is also good for expanding the awareness to higher levels.

Tourmaline

Tourmaline is one of the very special New Age stones. Like quartz, it possesses piezoelectric properties. One of the most beautiful of stones, tourmaline forms in the trigonal system as long striated crystals and can be found in many parts of the world. Tourmaline is the name given to the family which includes achroite (colourless), dravite (brown), indicolite (blue), rubellite (pink to red), siberite (lilac), verdelite (green) and schorl (black).

Tourmaline is the stone of protection. It wards off fear and negativity and protects on all levels. The different coloured tourmalines are wonderful stones to use with the corresponding chakras so it is not surprising that in this day and age many people are drawn to tourmaline. Its protective energies instil confidence, enhancing understanding and inspiration.

70

Turquoise

This beautiful vibrant blue-green stone has been much prized. As long ago as 1,000 years Native Americans began mining turquoise in New Mexico. The name, meaning 'Turkish Stone', was given to it by the French as this Persian stone first arrived in Europe via the trade route through Turkey. Turquoise forms in the triclinic system as large masses and veins.

The colour can vary from green to sky-blue. The very intense deep blue colour is the rarest and the most highly sought after. The colour of turquoise is not stable and will change when subjected to light, heat, perspiration, etc. The majority of turquoise on the market today is stabilised with oil, paraffin or an acrylic solution. Pure turquoise is rare. Most pieces will contain turquoise matrix, which is composed of veins of limonite (brown), sandstone (dark grey), or jasper or psilomelane (black). The main source of turquoise is the south-western USA.

Turquoise balances and protects — Native Americans carried it both for protection and good luck — blue turquoise symbolised Heaven, green turquoise symbolised Earth. It has a calming influence which brings peace of mind and understanding, instilling wisdom and loyalty. Turquoise enhances psychic abilities and aids communication and creativity.

The Fantasy Crystals

Elsewhere in this book when we speak of fakes and forgeries (see page 82) we are talking of stones that have been altered to 'impersonate' something else, usually a stone of greater value — for example, dyed howlite for turquoise, glass for clear quartz, plastic for amber.

Since the eighteenth century chemical science has attempted to produce copies of crystals and minerals. Synthetic gemstones have been perfected to an extent where it takes laboratory testing to define their 'true' nature. Stones are dyed to enhance their original colour and unnaturally large gemstones are created. With all of these stones the emphasis is on illusion. However, no matter how good a copy will appear to be, it will never replace the real thing.

In recent times a process has been developed using clear quartz and gold which has succeeded in bringing a new dimension to the stone. In the process, which allows molecules of pure gold to adhere to the natural electric charge which surrounds clear quartz, a new fantasy crystal has been born. Its name is aqua aura. The fine, transparent layer of gold over the stone breaks light into its spectral colours and the clear quartz appears a brilliant, vibrant turquoise-blue colour.

Aqua aura holds both the properties of clear quartz and also of gold. It is a beautiful stone to wear as it stimulates the throat chakra.

The other fantasy crystal recently born in the laboratory is aurora quartz. The process which creates this stone uses titanium. It is not restricted to just clear quartz, and can be used on other stones. The spectacular result is an opaque crystal of intense metallic colour in which every face can be different to show deep blue, gold and magenta. However, unlike aqua aura, which retains the 'feel' of clear quartz, we personally find that the process which creates aurora quartz, though it produces a visually beautifully stone, somehow overwhelms the crystal.

You may or may not be attracted to fantasy crystals. Their beauty is undeniable and they certainly never go unnoticed. While they do have a place in the crystal world, your decision is a personal one.

Stones from Outer Space

There has always been much fascination with these visitors from space. So many try to come, yet so very few arrive they are indeed gifts from other worlds. Many different theories exist as to their origins.

Meteorites

Every day thousands of solid bodies enter the Earth's atmosphere, most of which are burnt up. Only a very few survive to fall to the Earth's

76

surface. These are called meteorites. In the past, many cultures have considered these fiery visitors to be sacred stones sent from the heavens.

There are three groups of meteorites which are distinguished by their mineralogical make-up — the irons (comprised mainly of nickel and iron), the chondrites (stone) and the very rare achondrites (comprised of stone and/or olivine crystals).

The energies of these stones enhance our awareness and it is thought that they facilitate communication with extraterrestrials and can assist us in the remembering and understanding of past lives. Meteorite serves to balance both physical and non-physical bodies.

Tektites

The other travellers that come to us from space are tektites. These fascinating objects are meteoritic glass, usually no bigger than 3 centimetres (1 inch) in size. Tektites are found in only a few places on Earth and are named after the area they are found — Australites from Australia and Javaites from Java, for example. The majority of tektites have been found in the Philippines. They are mostly black, with the exception of moldavite, from Czechoslovakia, which is green.

As with meteorites, the energies of tektites are focussed towards extraterrestrial awareness and communication. They balance the yin–yang energies and increase the energy field.

CHAPTER FOUR

A Pocketful of Stones

What are Crystals for?

For those new to the world of crystals the question often asked is, what do I do with them? — how do I use crystals? For many people just having the crystals around them and enjoying their beauty is enough. Although they may not realise it, they are benefiting from their presence — there is a reason that the stones have come to them. More and more people are carrying stones and using crystals in a variety of different ways. Remember, as with the choosing of your stones, always go with what 'feels right' for you.

Wearing Crystals

Gemstones have been worn and carried for centuries by many different cultures. Precious and semi-precious stones were set in rings, necklaces, bracelets and crowns, and swords and breastplates were embellished with gems. The use of gemstones was not just for adornment — their influence and healing properties have long been recognised. In modern-day western countries gemstones have mainly been worn both as a symbol of wealth and as adornments of beauty. However, with the dawn of the New Age we are once again

Clear quartz sphere, rose quartz generator and wand from Brazil
with destiny stones

recognising the intrinsic value of these stones. There is a wide range of beautiful crystal jewellery available today, or you may like to take that special crystal and have it set in your own unique design. What better way to keep your crystals close than to wear them?

Choosing a Crystal

How do I choose a crystal — by size or colour, or shape? What about cost? And how will I know that it's the right one for me?

Crystals will come to you in many different ways. They may be given to you as a gift. You may find one, in the most unlikely of places. They may be forgotten childhood treasures tucked away in the corner of the attic or set in jewellery in Grandma's trinket box. Most often, though, you will obtain your crystals by buying them.

These days there are many New Age book stores and crystal shops offering a wide selection of crystals of every shape and size from which to choose. Shopping for crystals is a wonderful experience, so relax and trust in your feelings — just as you will find the right crystal, so the right crystal will find you. So often the first one that catches your eye will be the one. The shop owner will understand that crystals need to be touched, so don't be afraid to ask if you can hold and inspect different stones.

You will encounter a wide price range. The price of the crystal will depend upon its type, quality and size. Pieces such as spheres, wands and pyramids will have been cut and carefully polished by hand. The cutting and grinding of stones is a time-consuming craft, so you must expect to pay more for hand-worked pieces. The colour, clarity and condition of the crystal will determine its quality. This is something that you will soon determine by comparing prices. But always remember that with crystal energy (as with us!), beauty is in the eye of the beholder, so choose from the heart.

Some people prefer a crystal to be in its natural form while others prefer cut and polished shapes. You may set out to buy a clear quartz cluster, yet find that it is a polished amethyst pyramid, a piece of black tourmaline or just a small tumbled stone that you cannot resist.

Hold the crystal in your hand, clear your mind and focus on the feel of the stone — it may feel cold or warm, or you may feel a tingling sensation. The energies of every stone will be different. Don't worry if you can't feel anything — you may just be trying too hard or it may not be the right crystal for you. Relax — trust your inner feelings in the selection of your stones. You will know which stones are meant for you. If you are buying a crystal for a specific purpose affirm that purpose as you look at the stones.

Lead Crystal

There is often confusion over the name, especially since the resurgence of interest in crystal balls. Originally created in Austria, lead crystal is man-made glass which contains a high percentage of lead. It gained worldwide popularity when made into chandeliers, drinking glasses and decanters. Unfortunately, in recent times lead crystal balls and jewellery have sometimes been sold as 'real crystal' — knowingly or unknowingly — by some retailers.

When placed in direct sunlight faceted Austrian lead crystal casts rainbow spectra. If you have a window in your home that takes direct sunlight, then suspend a piece of lead crystal in it. The lead crystal will dapple the room with a myriad of brilliantly coloured rainbows.

Of Fakes and Forgeries

Whilst most people are aware that imitation diamonds and coloured glass stones are set in costume jewellery they usually assume that crystals and crystal jewellery are the 'real thing'. Some stones, such as agate, dye very well and often a stone's natural beauty can be dramatically enhanced by colour. The brightly coloured agate bookends, pyramids, etc., that you see in shops are all dyed, for example. We have nothing against dyed stones — indeed, it is sometimes the initial attraction to a dyed stone that introduces a person to crystals. If you choose to wear dyed or fake crystal, that is your choice. However, we do believe that you should know what it is that you are buying.

When shopping for crystals we suggest you go to a reputable retailer. Never be afraid to question the authenticity of a stone. Once you are familiar with handling crystals your instinct will often let you know if a stone is not what it seems to be.

However, there are a number of things to watch out for. Glass, for example, is sometimes substituted for clear quartz. With practice, you should be able to tell the difference because genuine clear quartz will have a sparkle and crispness that glass can never possess. When buying clear quartz jewellery the stone should feel cold when held to your cheek. Beware, too, of machine-cut stones. You can identify these in jewellery as every one will be the same size, and completely clear. Lapis lazuli and turquoise are two of the most impersonated stones. The stone often dyed to imitate them is white howlite. In large pieces the fake would be quite obvious but small stones set in jewellery are not so easily detected by the novice. Lead crystal and green glass are sometimes misleadingly called clear and green obsidian. And amber can be faked right down to the insect inclusions!

We could say much more about synthetic and dyed stones, but these are the most common things to beware of in New Age shops.

Rutilated quartz sphere from Brazil

Cleansing Your Crystal

Crystals absorb and retain energies and vibrations and it is for this reason that it is important to cleanse all your crystals thoroughly. The crystal may have been handled by many different people, so your first step should be to clear any negative energies that it may have retained.

There are various methods for cleansing crystals and stones but it is important that you choose the method that 'feels right' for you. Whichever method you choose it should be done with love and respect for the stones. The cleansing of your crystal is an important ritual, so choose a place where you will be undisturbed and where you will feel completely at ease. Take time, relax your body and clear your mind. Imagine yourself surrounded by pure white light, then focus your mind upon the crystal. The intent of what you are doing is as important as the action. Always keep your focus upon the cleansing of the stone.

With Water

Take your crystal to natural running water — the ocean, a river or stream. Hold the crystal in the water and visualise the water washing the negativity away. Hold it in the water for several minutes or until you feel that the crystal has been cleansed.

With Salt

Buy a bag of sea salt from your local health food store and, depending upon the size of the crystal, fill a glass dish or bowl with enough salt so that you can completely bury the stone. The salt will absorb all the negativity. Leave for three days, then remove the crystal and rinse with pure water.

With Incense

This is what Native Americans call 'smudging' (meaning 'to fill an area with smoke'). The best incense to use for this purpose is frankincense, but cedar and sage may also be used. Focus upon the cleansing ritual and as you pass your crystal through the smoke, visualise the crystal being purified.

In Earth

Choose a place in your garden to dig a hole deep enough to bury your crystal in. The perfect place may be at the base of a large tree or in a favourite spot.

As you dig your hole and bury your crystal, visualise the earth drawing the negative energies from the stone. Leave for three days, then retrieve the crystal and rinse with pure water.

With White Light

Holding the crystal in your right hand, visualise a stream of pure white light entering through the top of your head and flowing down through your body to your hands and from your hands to the crystal. Visualise the white light purifying the crystal.

Note: When choosing a method to cleanse crystal jewellery where the setting may have been glued, or when cleansing stones of a porous nature, it is not advisable to use the water or earth method.

Caring for Your Crystals

The crystals that come into your life will bring you much happiness and joy, so you will want to take good care of them. Crystals love to be looked at, so don't keep them locked away in a dark cupboard. Keep them clean and dust-free; crystals such as amethyst and clear quartz love water and will sparkle when washed and then dried with a soft cloth.

Crystals also love sunlight, so place your crystals outside in the sun for half an hour and the solar rays will energise them. A word of warning, though — it is not advisable to leave coloured stones in direct sunlight for long periods of time as over-exposure can gradually fade the colours of some stones. Remember that some types of stones can be quite fragile, too, and that points can become chipped and broken if dropped or knocked. Always handle your crystals with love and care and they will remain your friends for life.

Creating a Sacred Space

With the following processes and meditations it is important to create an atmosphere of harmony and peace. To do this you should choose somewhere where you will not be disturbed and where you will feel relaxed and safe. You may prefer to subdue the light or work with candlelight. You may also wish to make a special place to display your crystals and stones.

Take time for yourself — you may like to bathe first and wash away all traces of the hustle and bustle of the outside world. Light some candles and, as you do, affirm that you are creating this space with love and respect. Burning incense or essential oils will also increase the harmony of the room. You may choose to play some relaxing background music. Sit in the centre of the room, close your eyes and visualise a cloud of brilliant white light encompassing the whole room. Affirm that this is your sacred place. You may prefer to find a place in nature — a forest or seashore. Wherever you choose to be, know that you are capable of creating that special space.

Programming Crystals

A clear quartz crystal can be programmed with a thought or the intent to use it for a specific purpose. For example, you may be worried about taking an exam. Take a cleansed clear quartz crystal and sit quietly, holding the crystal. Close your eyes, relax your body and clear your mind. Bring a focus to your breathing — breathe slow, deep breaths — and with every breath you will become calmer and more relaxed. Imagine a waterfall of white light washing over you. Hold the terminated point of the crystal to your third eye. Imagine yourself going into the exam room, relaxed and confident, knowing that you will excel. Visualise these thoughts flowing into and remaining in the crystal. Carry the crystal with you and know that it will project back your programmed thoughts to you.

Touch Stones

When we were children most of us at some stage had a collection of pebbles or river stones. As adults many people rediscover this fascination and touch, or tumbled stones have become increasingly popular. Tumbled stones are pieces of crystal or stone that have been rotated in a revolving drum with finer and finer grades of sand until they are smooth and shiny.

Tumbled stones are ideal to carry with you as their smooth, rounded contours make them less likely to be damaged. When choosing tumbled stones, as with choosing any crystal, rely on your feelings. What you instinctively choose is always the stone you need most. The stones are happy to be together, so if you wish to carry them with you, a soft drawstring pouch is ideal.

Citrine

The stone for abundance. Pop a few small pieces of tumbled citrine into your purse or wallet, and it will never be empty.

Hematite

A stone good for relieving stress. If you feel that you will be placed in a stressful situation, carry a piece of hematite in your pocket.

Fluorite

An ideal stone to assist in studying and to take into the exam room as it aids concentration.

These are just a few stones which can assist you in different situations. (See the Crystal and Mineral Guide on pages 112 to 123 for more information.)

Friendship Stones

Friendship stones are small agate geodes that are hollow inside. Geodes come in many shapes and sizes and each one is unique. These enchanting stones that are quite ordinary on the outside often conceal beautiful crystal formations within and when cut in half form two crystal caves. The energy that links the two halves can never be broken. You can programme these stones and use their energy to form a link with someone you love. As you make your selection, hold the image of that special person in your mind.

To use your friendship stone, first thoroughly cleanse the geode. The following process is very special and not something you should rush. Go to your sacred space. Holding the two halves of the geode together, visualise a stream of pure brilliant white light entering through the top of your head and travelling down through your heart chakra to your hands. Visualise that very special friend or lover. Imagine all your loving thoughts and feelings for that person flowing from your heart chakra to the geode. Know that all those thoughts and feelings have joined with the energies in the stone. Then take the two halves of the geode and choose the half you feel is appropriate and give it to that special person as a token of your love and affection. The half that you have chosen to keep you will treasure for ever.

Destiny Stones

The answers you seek you already have — everything that you desire is within you to achieve.

Crystals and stones can be used as a guidance to your inner wisdom. So often we look outside for answers when in fact all we need to do is

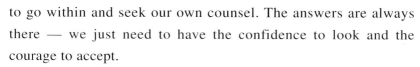

Agate geode from Brazil

to go within and seek our own counsel. The answers are always there — we just need to have the confidence to look and the courage to accept.

For this exercise we have chosen twelve different stones. You will need a pouch or bag in which to keep the stones, large enough to easily put your hand into. As you collect your destiny stones together you may decide to include others. Any combination or number of stones can be used. Most people prefer to keep their destiny stones for their own personal use as they will become attuned to the stones' energies.

Whenever you have a problem or a decision to make, use the stones to guide you. Go to your sacred space, take time, relax. Close your eyes, clear your mind, focus only upon the question at hand. Reach into the bag and draw out a stone.

Focus upon the stone that you have selected, consider the properties of the stone in relation to your question, trust your feelings and instincts. If the answer does not come at once, carry the stone with you and consider the question during the course of the day.

The answer will come, and you will recognise it as right and true. Trust your inner wisdom, have the courage to be the master of your own destiny.

Amethyst

A stone of great spirituality. The emphasis here is on calmness, peace, love and understanding.

Aquamarine

A stone of courage. Also to do with clear thinking, communication and self-expression.

Aventurine

A stone of independence. The emphasis here is on positive attitudes and decisiveness.

Carnelian

A stone of concentration. To do with dispelling apathy and stimulating activity.

Clear Quartz

A stone of great energy. The emphasis here is on positive actions.

Hematite

A stone for stress. The emphasis here is on calming down and thinking things through.

Jade

A stone of harmony. To do with wisdom, clarity and understanding.

Moonstone

A stone of the emotions. The emphasis here is on understanding and not over-reacting.

Rhodonite

A stone of the heart. To do with self-esteem and having confidence in yourself.

Rose Quartz

A stone of love. The emphasis here is on calming emotions and soothing jealousies.

Sodalite

A stone of clarity. To do with self-expression and communication on all levels.

Tiger Eye

A stone of perception. The emphasis here is on balance and understanding.

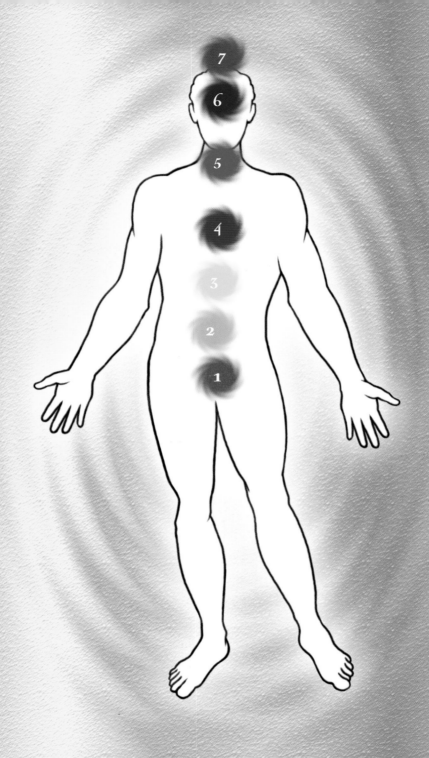

The Chakras

In an age when so much importance is placed upon health, diet and exercise we must also learn to care for our 'invisible' self. Working with the chakras is just as important as working on the physical body. Just as, when neglected, the wheels and cogs of a machine can slow and become unbalanced, so the chakras need to be cared for and kept in 'good working order'. As we begin to understand and learn, so all aspects of our lives will improve and flourish.

To understand the chakras, which are also known as lotuses, we must first understand that just as we have a physical body so we also have an etheric body. It is within that subtle body that the chakras are located, and it is the chakras that form the bridge between the physical and the non-physical self.

A chakra, from the Sanskrit word meaning 'wheel', is a spinning vortex of energy. These wheels can spin slowly or quickly, depending on the degree of energy in the system. There are seven major chakras, each one corresponding to a different physical system and its related organs, and to each of the endocrine glands. The health of the physical body mirrors the 'health' of the chakras. Each chakra also corresponds to one of the colours of the rainbow spectrum and to the crystals and stones that relate to that particular colour ray.

First: Base

Situated at the base of the spine, this chakra connects us to our roots. It relates to the large intestine, rectum, legs, feet and adrenal glands. The colour is red. The stones are red jasper, red garnet, ruby, bloodstone, black tourmaline, obsidian, smoky quartz and black onyx.

Second: Sacral

This chakra is located just below the naval and governs sexuality. It relates to the reproductive system, kidneys, ovaries and testicles. The colour is orange. The stones are carnelian, amber and orange calcite.

Third: Solar Plexus

The solar plexus chakra governs basic health and is found in the middle of the abdomen. It is where our 'gut feeling' comes from. It relates to the stomach, liver, digestive system, small intestine and pancreas. The colour is yellow. The stones are citrine, yellow topaz, tiger eye and yellow calcite.

Fourth: Heart

Positioned in the middle of the chest, this is the chakra of love and compassion. It relates to the heart, lungs, chest, arms and thymus gland. The colour is green. The stones are aventurine, chrysoprase, emerald, malachite, peridot and green tourmaline, and the pink (heart) stones pink tourmaline, rose quartz and kunzite.

98

Fifth: Throat

This chakra is to do with communication and expression. It relates to the throat, voice, neck, shoulders and thyroid gland. The colour is bright blue. The stones are aquamarine, turquoise, amazonite, blue lace agate, chrysocolla and blue topaz.

Sixth: Brow

Located just above the bridge of the nose, this is the third eye chakra. It relates to vision, the higher brain centres and the pituitary gland. The colour is indigo. The stones are lapis lazuli, azurite, sodalite and sapphire.

Seventh: Crown

Located at the top of the head this is the chakra of spirituality. It relates to the highest brain centres, the pineal gland and to the whole body. The colour is violet. The stones are amethyst, fluorite, clear quartz and diamond.

A White Light Exercise

Stand with your feet apart, your weight evenly balanced, in a comfortable standing position. Relax your body and clear your mind. Breathe deeply and with every outward breath be aware of the ground beneath your feet, your connection to the earth, and how right it feels.

Visualise a cascade of brilliant pure white light washing over you from the top of your head to the tips of your toes.

In your right hand take a clear quartz crystal and hold it several centimetres away from your body, the point facing towards you, in line with the base (first) chakra. Focusing upon that chakra, visualise a stream of pure white light flowing from the tip of the crystal to the chakra. Slowly rotate the crystal clockwise, visualising the spinning wheel of white light energy at the base of your spine. In your own time repeat the process with each of the chakras in turn. Finally, visualise all the chakras — seven brilliant spinning catherine wheels of pure energy.

Know that your chakras have been cleared and activated. Feel the vitality surging through your physical body.

A Colour Meditation

Lie down on your back in a comfortable position and place one or more of the corresponding stones on top of your body in line with each chakra. If you wish, you may also place a clear quartz crystal above your head or next to any of the stones to amplify their energy.

Close your eyes, and relax your body and mind. Imagine yourself enveloped in a cloud of brilliant pure white light. In your own time, focus upon the base (first) chakra. Think the colour red, see the colour red, *be* the colour red. Visualise the base chakra — a spinning vibrant vortex of red energy. Keep your focus upon the base of your spine; imagine that fiery wheel — the red of rubies, fire-engine red, blood red. Visualise the energies of the stone enhancing the energies of the chakra.

When you are ready, move your focus to each chakra in turn. Enjoy the kaleidoscope of colour as you move upwards to the crown. Finally, from out of the cloud of brilliant white light visualise the entire rainbow bridge, each spinning in a dazzling vortex of colour.

In your own time, bring your mind back and slowly open your eyes. Know that your chakras have been activated and enlivened and your energies charged. The memories of the breathtaking colours of your meditation will reflect around you as you go through your day.

Note on choosing crystals for chakra work: For the white light exercise you may find that a large clear quartz natural point works best for you; however, a polished clear quartz wand could also be used. For the colour meditation see the Crystal and Mineral Guide (Chapter 5) to find out more about the individual stones. They may be in their unworked form, tumbled or cabochon (domed), but it is wise to choose stones with a flattish side so that they won't roll away during the meditation.

Using a Crystal Pendulum

Dowsing — searching for minerals and water using a divining rod — is an ancient art which has often mystified and always fascinated. You can adapt this technique, using crystals, to search for answers to issues that are important to you. A clear quartz crystal makes a perfect dowsing instrument. You will be able to buy a crystal pendulum from many New Age shops though many people prefer to select and make their own.

To make a pendulum you will need a crystal, preferably one that is symmetrical and not too heavy — about 3 to 4 centimetres (1 to 1½ inches) long — and a silver chain approximately 25 centimetres (10 inches) long to suspend it from. If you choose a crystal that is not already set, you will need to wrap silver wire around the top to enable you to attach the chain.

As a pendulum can only give yes or no answers the first thing to establish is how it swings for each. To do this, hold the end of the chain between the thumb and first finger of your right hand and hold the pendulum over the palm of your left hand.

Ask an easy yes question — for example, 'Is today's date ——?' The pendulum will start to circle either clockwise or anti-clockwise. To confirm the direction of the yes swing, now ask a definite no question and the pendulum should swing in the opposite direction.

The direction of the yes and no swings usually remains the same. However, at the start of a pendulum session it is a good idea to ask a definite yes or no question as the direction has been known to change. Should the pendulum swing back and forth rather than circle it means that the question does not have a definite yes or no answer at that time.

The pendulum can also be used held out in front of you (with your arm at a 45-degree angle). It can be held over objects or lists and questioned and can assist you in the selection of your crystals. As with all things, be guided by your inner knowing.

Working with a pendulum takes practice. At first you may be too tense or you may find yourself swinging the pendulum from side to side. Be patient, persevere — the fun and intrigue you will gain is well worth it.

Channelling

To use a crystal to channel, it is important that you are aware of the seriousness of what you are doing. It is not something to do flippantly because when you open up to channel you are exposing yourself to unseen entities who may or may not work in your best interests. It is vital that you protect yourself from lower entities who may draw on your energy.

Before opening to channel, sit quietly in your sacred space and contemplate what it is you are about to do. Make sure that you protect yourself and your surroundings with white light (see pages 99–100). Affirm that the information that you receive will be from highly evolved beings who are there to help you. Ask for protection and guidance.

In your own time, visualise your throat and third eye (fifth and sixth) chakras. Visualise the brilliant blue and indigo light emanating from these two chakras. As you do this, affirm once again that you are protected and will be guided. Take the crystal and hold the seven-sided face to your third eye and bring your focus to that chakra. Allow the images, messages and feelings to come. Do not try to analyse or question — just allow yourself to accept.

Crystal Ball Gazing

Crystal balls have long been synonymous with fortune-telling and seeing into the future. However, the stereotype of the coin-clad fairground gypsy muttering over her crystal ball has often led to ridicule and misconception of the use of crystal balls.

Crystal balls are available from marble-size upwards, but if you wish to use a ball for crystal gazing then you will need one of a reasonable size. Most crystal balls will not be completely clear. Indeed, be wary of large, completely clear balls as, unless they are extremely expensive, they will not be natural quartz crystal but man-

made lead crystal. (These balls can be used as a focus, just as the flame of a candle can be used in this way, but they can never have the energies that natural clear quartz possesses.)

Every crystal ball is different. Some are like fantastic crystal galaxies, others resemble glacial formations and often show beautiful rainbows. You will find that your crystal ball will become very special to you and will be an important part of your crystal collection.

The ball is used as a focus and its very nature makes it the ideal tool for this. Crystal-ball gazing is an ideal way of increasing your psychic powers and opening the third eye. It is also a beautiful focus to use for meditation.

Choose a comfortable seated position. The crystal ball can be cupped in the palms of your hands or placed on a table in front of you. Lovingly create your special space, relax your body and clear your mind. Bring your focus to the crystal ball. You may find after a few minutes that your eyes start to water or smart and that you need to look away. Don't worry —it just means that you are straining too hard. With a little practice you will become used to gazing into the ball and once this happens you will relax and your mind will open. Trust the images that you see and the impressions that come to you — the crystal ball is reflecting your psychic awareness. As your psychic abilities increase, practise upon a friend. Place the ball upon the table between you, gaze into the crystal, focussing your thoughts through the ball to the other person. Trust in yourself — you are capable of doing this. Your crystal ball can also be used at the beginning of a meditation to relax and clear your mind. It can then, if you wish, be held for the rest of the meditation.

Crystal Drinking Water

A clear quartz crystal can be used to enhance the flavour of drinking water. To do this, thoroughly cleanse and wash a small piece of clear quartz; a short natural point is ideal. However, be careful not to use anything too heavy as you do not want to damage either the crystal or the jug as you pour. Place it into a glass jug or container filled with water. Leave for 24 hours and then taste the difference in the water. The crystal can be left permanently in your water jug.

Crystals and Plants

It is not only you who can benefit from having crystals near you — plants will also benefit if you place a clear quartz crystal in the soil around them. If you are repotting a plant, place a small crystal in the bottom of the pot. Plants love the crystal energies and you will notice the difference as the plant grows and flourishes. If you don't want to bury the crystal, place it on top of the soil. Its close proximity to the plant will still have some effect.

Fresh cut flowers will also last longer if you leave a clear quartz crystal in their vase. Don't forget to cleanse the crystal when you change the water.

Crystal Healing and the Laying-on of Stones

We have spoken in previous chapters of the healing energies of crystals. In an age in which technology has taken us into space and computer science formats our daily lives it seems surprising that sickness and disease have not been combated to a greater degree. Perhaps we should look at the word disease, or dis-ease. In a society where it is so easy to take a pill to stop pain, to cheer you up, to calm you down, why are so many people turning to alternative healing practices? Is it because they are not at ease with everything that modern medicine promotes? Whilst there is no denying the achievements of today's medicine, perhaps Nature's wisdom has been too long ignored. Are we only treating the result when we should be treating the cause?

Stress is a twentieth-century plague — or is it? Can office politics or city driving be more stressful than our distant ancestors' struggle for survival against wild animals and warring tribes? We think not. Is it not more likely that we have allowed our life energies to slow, that we have lost our way in the technology jungle?

From the day we are born we store up emotions: anger, frustration, jealousy, grief. Often we bring trauma and unresolved experiences from past lives into this life. By the time we reach maturity the burden of stored-up emotions can be so great it can overwhelm. Unfortunately, these emotions are sometimes so deeply buried that we cannot see them and so they are carried through life and never resolved. These can be transmuted into disease.

The New Age movement heralds a time of enlightenment and many new (and often, very old) healing techniques are being used by New Age healers. The underlying message is that to heal the physical body the spiritual body must also be healed. So frequently it is the will that heals the body. Sadly, the lack of will sometimes lets it die.

The use of crystals in healing is indeed an ancient art. The crystal healers of today are working with potent tools that have been universally recognised down through the centuries. We have talked in this book of the Earth energy, the crystal energy and the energies within us. It is on these levels that crystal healing takes place.

The laying-on of stones allows the energies of the crystals to activate the energies within the auric field. The crystal energies connect within the energies of the subtle body and act as a catalyst in releasing blockages, dispelling negativity and aligning and balancing the energy centres.

A crystal healing can involve placing literally dozens of stones upon the body, and the charge of energy that can occur as a result can be quite dramatic. The healing that takes place does so at a deep level, reaching to the very essence of your being. The energies are undeniable. However, you must be prepared to take responsibility for your own wellbeing, to face and release that storehouse of emotion and to reach down to the very core. Only with that acceptance of responsibility can come spiritual growth.

CHAPTER FIVE

A Crystal and Mineral Guide

The following guide covers over 70 different minerals and crystals.

Colour: an indication of the usual colour of the stone. However, some stones occur in a range of shades: an amethyst, for example, can vary from the palest lilac to the deepest purple. Where we have stated 'various', that stone occurs in a range of different colours.

Star sign: every stone relates to one or more signs of the zodiac. If you are looking for a zodiac-aligned crystal and you are born, for example, under the sign of Sagittarius, you may feel drawn to the blue stones such as azurite, lapis lazuli and turquoise or the beautiful greys of labradorite and smoky quartz.

Chakra: the stones also relate to one or more of the chakras. Where both colour and chakra are described as 'various', the actual colour of your own stone will suggest the chakra. For example, you might own a black tourmaline, which would correspond to the first (base) chakra.

Qualities: a brief description of the energies of each stone.

♈	♉	♊	♋	♌	♍
Aries	*Taurus*	*Gemini*	*Cancer*	*Leo*	*Virgo*
♎	♏	♐	♑	♒	♓
Libra	*Scorpio*	*Sagittarius*	*Capricorn*	*Aquarius*	*Pisces*

Amethyst 'cave' with semi-precious stones

Crystal	Colour	System	Star sign
Agate	various	trigonal	♊
Alexandrite	green	orthorhombic	♏
Amazonite	turquoise-blue	triclinic	♍
Amber	golden-yellow	amorphous	♌ ♒
Amertrine	purple & yellow	trigonal	♎
Amethyst	purple	trigonal	♓ ♍ ♒ ♑
Apatite	various	hexagonal	♊
Apophyllite	white/pale green	tetragonal	♎ ♊
Aquamarine	light blue	hexagonal	♊ ♓ ♈
Aragonite	various	orthorhombic	♑
Aventurine	green	trigonal	♈
Azurite	deep blue	monoclinic	♐

Chakra	Quality
various	The strength stone. Courage and strength for both body and mind. Facilitates perceptiveness and precision. Is grounding yet energetic and powerful. Assists in balancing the yin–yang energies.
4th/7th	Aligns and balances mentally, physically and emotionally. Aids spiritual transformation and regeneration.
5th	Aligns and balances the physical with the etheric body. Calms nerves, aids creative expression and soothes the emotions. Brings joy, clarity and an understanding of universal love.
3rd/7th	Harmonious and soothing. Absorbs and turns negative energy into positive energy. Calming and cheering influences. Enlivens body and mind.
7th	Combines the properties of amethyst and citrine.
7th	The peace stone. Ideal for meditation and enhancing psychic abilities. It has a great calming and comforting influence. Very protective and inspirational. Radiates divine love.
various	Enhances creativity, balances the emotions and stimulates the intellect. Enhances clairvoyant abilities.
4th/7th	Aids in the connection with higher dimensions. An excellent stone to use for astral travel.
5th	Provides emotional and intellectual stability and clarity of mind and inspiration. Aids self-expression, calms nerves, dispels intolerance and helps banish fears, doubts and phobias.
various	Calms and reduces stress and cools hot tempers. Enhances reliability, instils patience and encourages sensibility.
4th	Balances the yin–yang energies. Motivates and refines positive attitudes and feelings of independence. Relieves anxiety and fear.
6th	Cleanses the mind and soul. Awakens psychic abilities and initiates transformation. Enhances creativity, self-confidence and inspiration.

Crystal	Colour	System	Star sign
Bloodstone (heliotrope)	dark green with red flecks	trigonal	a l g
Calcite	various	trigonal	d
Carnelian	orange to red	trigonal	b d e
Celestite	blue	orthorhombic	c
Chlorite	green	monoclinic	i
Chrysocolla (gem silica)	blue-green	amorphous	c f
Chrysoprase	apple-green	trigonal	g
Citrine	yellow	trigonal	c a e
Clear quartz	colourless	trigonal	all
Copper	golden-red	cubic	b i
Coral	various	hexagonal	l
Diamond	colourless	cubic	a e b
Dioptase	emerald-green	trigonal	i h

Chakra	Quality
1st/4th	A powerful healing stone of renewal. Revitalises and enhances both body and mind. Instils wisdom and sensitivity for inner guidance.
various	Facilitates an awareness and understanding of nature. Aids in the remembering of astral travel experiences. Alleviates fear, clears and balances.
2nd	Aids concentration and memory. Stimulates inquisitiveness and dispels apathy. Enhances attunement with the inner self.
5th	Good for communication, clear speech and creative expression. Brings harmony, peace and balance.
all	Emits positive energies, calms and balances on all levels. Purifies and cleanses the aura and chakras.
4th/5th	A very feminine stone. Balances the emotions and eases heartache and tension. Brings out inner strengths.
4th	Instils a sense of grace. Helps clarify personal problems and brings out hidden talents. Balances attitudes and actions.
3rd	The abundance stone. Joyous, warm and energising. Raises self-esteem, stimulates mental focus and aids in the alignment with the higher self. Attracts and maintains abundance.
7th	The energy stone. Excellent for meditation. Amplifies energy and thought. Dispels negativity. Receives, stores and transmits energy. Aids communication with every dimension.
1st/3rd/4th	Energises and balances body and mind. An excellent stone to combat lethargy and tiredness.
1st/4th/5th	Calms the emotions and aids communication and understanding. Allows for a balanced outlook.
7th	Purity, trust, innocence and faithfulness. Enhances energies of the mind, body and spirit on the highest levels.
4th	Calms and balances and brings emotional stability and a feeling of wellbeing.

Crystal	Colour	System	Star sign
Emerald	bright green	hexagonal	♉ ♊ ♈
Fluorite	various	cubic	♓ ♑
Galena	metallic grey	cubic	♑
Garnet	red/various	cubic	♍ ♑ ♒
Gold	gold	cubic	♌
Hematite	metallic grey	trigonal	♈ ♒
Herkimer diamond	colourless	trigonal	♐
Howlite	white	monoclinic	♊
Jade	green	monoclinic	♈ ♊ ♎
Jasper	various	trigonal	♌
Jet	black	amorphous	♑
Kunzite	pink	monoclinic	♏ ♉ ♌
Kyanite	blue to colourless	triclinic	♉ ♎ ♈

Chakra	Quality
4th	Love and harmony. Stimulates positive actions and wards off negativity. Enhances spiritual insight and the ability to remember dreams.
various	Balances and advances the mind and increases concentration. A stabilising influence on all levels. A stone of discernment and higher understanding.
1st	Grounds and centres the physical and non-physical body. Opens the mind to higher thinking.
1st/4th	A stone of love and compassion. It strengthens and purifies, balances the body's energy field and enhances the imagination.
3rd/4th/7th	Brings positive energies and balances the energy field. Enhances and mentally stimulates.
1st	Enhances mental capabilities and is excellent for reducing stress. Strengthens and energises both physical and etheric bodies. Dispels negativity and encourages optimism.
all	Enhances inner vision and the remembering of dreams. Aids in reducing stress and relaxing body and mind.
5th	Reduces stress and pain and encourages patience, discernment and refinement. Aids communication and expression.
4th	Balances the emotions and encourages wisdom. Aids in remembering and solving dreams. Peaceful, nurturing and stress-relieving.
various	Protective and grounding, a balancer on all levels. A sustaining stone that works mainly on the physical body.
1st	Protective and calming influences on a physical level. Dispels fearful thoughts.
4th	Soothing and calming, a stone of the heart. Aids self-esteem and balances on all levels.
5th	Enhances communication and self expression, aligns and balances, bringing a calming tranquil influence.

Crystal	Colour	System	Starsign
Labradorite	dark grey	triclinic	♐ ♏ ♌
Lapis lazuli	deep blue	cubic	♐
Lepidolite	lilac/various	monoclinic	♎
Lodestone (magnetite)	black	cubic	♊ ♍
Malachite	green	monoclinic	♑ ♏
Meteorite	grey/varied	various	all
Moldavite	dark green	amorphous	♏
Moonstone	milky sheen	monoclinic	♋ ♎ ♏
Morganite	pink	hexagonal	♎
Obsidian	various	amorphous	♐
Onyx	various	trigonal	♌
Opal	various	amorphous	♋ ♎ ♓ ♏
Pearl	lustrous grey/white	amorphous	♋ ♊ ♓

Chakra	Quality
2nd	Encourages patience and perseverance and an understanding of inner knowing. Protects and balances the aura.
6th	Expands awareness and intellect and enhances psychic abilities. Protective, helps overcome depression and encourages creative expression.
4th	Uplifting and balancing, wards off depression. Enhances openness, honesty and self-love.
1st	Aligns and balances physical and non-physical bodies. Assists in aligning and activating chakras.
4th	Aids intuitiveness and transformation. Balances and revitalises, clarifies the emotions and helps clear subconscious blocks.
1st	Expands awareness, balances and aids communication with extraterrestrial energies. Assists in remembering past lives.
4th/6th	A stone from the stars. Aids in communication with extraterrestrial and interdimensional energies.
4th	Stimulates confidence and balances the emotions. Encourages intuitiveness and perception. Enhances the feminine nature.
4th	A stone of the heart, allowing love into your life. Assists in the understanding of relationships.
1st	Grounds, protects and shields against and absorbs negativity. Aids in the understanding and clearing of subconscious blocks.
various	Balances the yin–yang energies. Reduces stress and encourages self-control. Encourages happiness, good fortune and higher inspiration.
4th/various	Encourages intuitiveness, inspiration and imagination. Aids in memory improvement and in the releasing of inhibitions.
4th	Instils a sense of balance and grace. Pearls are a symbol of purity of both body and mind.

Crystal	Colour	System	Star sign
Peridot	green	orthorhombic	♍ ♌ ♐ ♏
Pyrite	gold	cubic	♌
Rhodochrosite	pink	trigonal	♏ ♌
Rhodonite	pink	triclinic	♉
Rose quartz	pink	trigonal	♉ ♎
Ruby	red	trigonal	♌ ♏ ♋
Rutilated quartz	clear with rutiles	trigonal	♊ ♉
Rutile	red/brown	tetragonal	♊ ♉
Sapphire	blue	trigonal	♍ ♎ ♐
Selenite (gypsum)	colourless	monoclinic	♉
Silver	silver	cubic	♒ ♋
Smoky quartz	grey/brown	trigonal	♑ ♐
Snowflake obsidian	black and white	amorphous	♍

Chakra	Quality
4th	Inspires happiness, strengthens and regenerates body and mind. Protects and purifies, reduces anger and jealousy.
1st	Protects against negativity on all levels. Encourages a positive outlook and greater understanding. Aids memory and intellect.
1st/4th	A stone of the heart. Balances and heals the emotions. Assists in attunement with the higher self.
1st/4th	Aids self-esteem and confidence. Reduces anxiety, balances, and inspires greater understanding and discernment. Assists in maximising potential.
4th	The love stone. Balances, heals and rejuvenates the emotions. Cools hot tempers, clears stored anger, guilt and jealousies. Encourages compassion and harmony.
1st/4th	Stimulates both the mind and the emotions. Protective and stabilising. A stone to invoke passion and enlightenment.
all	Combines the properties of rutile and clear quartz. Enhances insight and understanding of problems. Assists in communication with the higher self and guides.
1st	Stabilises and balances and wards off outside interference both mental and physical. Dispels negativity.
5th/6th	Inspirational, uplifting and joyful. Enhances communication and creative expression.
7th	Aids clear thinking and concentration and increases awareness on all levels.
1st	Balances the emotions and increases perception. Assists connection between physical and astral bodies. Improves speech.
1st	Dispels negativity and releases emotional blocks. Balances, grounds and protects. Enhances channelling powers.
1st	Brings purity and balance on all levels. Encourages understanding and realignment of thought patterns.

Crystal	Colour	System	Star sign
Sodalite	dark blue	cubic	♐
Sugilite	violet/pinkish purple	hexagonal	♍
Tanzanite	blue/violet	orthorhombic	♐ ♊ ♎
Tiger eye	golden/yellow/brown	trigonal	♑
Topaz	various	orthorhombic	♐
Tourmalinated quartz	clear/black	trigonal	♎
Tourmaline	various	trigonal	♎
Turquoise	blue-green	triclinic	♐ ♓ ♏
Unakite	green and pink	monoclinic	♏
Wulfenite	yellow/orange	tetragonal	♐
Zircon	various	tetragonal	♌ ♍ ♐

Chakra	Quality
6th	Rationalises and aids clear thinking, bringing clarity and truth. Enhances communication and creative expression.
6th/7th	Calms and balances the emotions, instiling a sense of freedom. Enhances understanding of life and increases spiritual awareness. An excellent stone for meditation.
5th/6th/7th	Enhances communication, awareness and psychic abilities. A stone for aspirations to higher levels.
2nd/3rd	Brings cheerfulness and optimism. Enhances clarity of thought, balances the yin–yang energies and helps soften stubbornness.
various	Enhances individuality, creativity and awareness. Aids confidence in decision-making and discourages negativity.
various	Combines the qualities of clear quartz and tourmaline. Aids in balancing extremes and eliminates destructive influences.
various	The protection stone. Wards off fear and negativity and protects on all levels. Enhances inspiration and encourages self-confidence and understanding.
5th	Brings peace of mind, wisdom and understanding. Enhances psychic abilities and communication. Protects and balances.
4th	Balances the emotions and gives an awareness and understanding of subconscious blocks. Can facilitate the rebirthing process.
2nd/3rd	A stone of rejuvenation on all levels. Enhances the understanding and communication with other planes.
all	Balances the emotions and enhances self esteem and unity. A stone of purity and innocence.

Index